TYNESIDE RAILWAYS

THE 1970s AND 1980s

Colin Alexander

AMBERLEY

First published 2016

Amberley Publishing
The Hill, Stroud
Gloucestershire, GL5 4EP

www.amberley-books.com

Copyright © Colin Alexander, 2016

The right of Colin Alexander to be identified
as the Author of this work has been asserted in
accordance with the Copyrights, Designs and
Patents Act 1988.

ISBN 978 1 4456 6230 5 (print)
ISBN 978 1 4456 6231 2 (ebook)

British Library Cataloguing in Publication Data.
A catalogue record for this book is available from
the British Library.

Typesetting by Amberley Publishing.
Printed in the UK.

Introduction

I was six years old when the 1960s gave way to the 1970s. Man had landed on the moon the year before, an event I remember watching on our old grainy black-and-white television. Although steam had ended on British Railways in 1968, my Dad would take me to see any steam 'special' that visited Newcastle, and many of the local industrial railways still relied on steam power. This book is intended to illustrate the many changes that took place both on the railways and in the North-East in general during a tumultuous twenty years, both for me and for Tyneside.

Tyneside is widely acknowledged as being at the epicentre of the birth of railways. Long before railway mania gripped Victorian Britain, pioneering engineers on both sides of the Tyne were connecting collieries to the river to facilitate the export of coal. Before this, coal had to be extracted close to navigable water, but the wooden wagon-ways of the 1700s allowed much more of the coalfield to be exploited. These primitive wagon-ways evolved into the 'iron road' and North-East men like William Hedley, William Chapman and, of course, George and Robert Stephenson were instrumental in replacing horsepower through the steam revolution that would shrink nations and continents across the world.

While the region had its glamorous Anglo-Scottish express passenger trains, the railways in the North-East were dominated by freight services, and the North Eastern Railway (NER) had a virtual monopoly from the Humber to the Scottish Border on the transport of vast amounts of coal, iron ore, steel, fish and other goods traffic for decades. This traffic continued after 1923 under the London & North Eastern Railway (LNER) and into the early days of post-war nationalisation in British Railways' North Eastern Region.

From the late 1970s onwards, the region went through a huge upheaval as Tyneside's traditional industries were decimated and the North-East's railways reflected that transition. Most of the area's industrial railways and freight lines closed and were lifted, while much of Newcastle's suburban passenger network, which had been in decline since the 1960s, was converted to the shiny new light rapid-transit Metro system, opening in 1980.

This twenty-year period, therefore, saw a huge transformation from an industrial Tyneside with essentially steam-age railway infrastructure to a clean electrified railway, serving a region almost devoid of any traditional industry. To show this transformation, I have placed the photographs in approximate chronological order.

I have tried to include as many locations as possible beyond Newcastle and Gateshead, visiting the suburbs and the beautiful Tyne Valley to the west, as well as going slightly further afield to locations in the South-East Northumberland coalfield and almost to Wearside.

I have tried to show a wide variety of motive power in the book, including preserved steam and BR diesel traction; steam, diesel and electric-powered industrial locomotives; Tyne & Wear Metro stock and even the ill-fated Advanced Passenger Train makes an unlikely appearance.

Recently, much of the North-East's rich railway heritage has seen a renaissance with some beautifully restored stations and bridges, and the region can boast some of the preservation movement's most precious relics.

This book tells the story of my own interest in local railways and history, but while many of the photographs are from my own camera, I quickly realised I had neither the variety nor the quality necessary to fill the book on my own.

Thanks must, therefore, go to my old friends Ian Beattie, David Tweddle, Neil Jordan, Craig Oliphant, Ian Robinson and Richard Vogel; along with Dave Jolly, Ernie Brack, George Woods, Marcus Gilmour, Trevor Casey, Geoff Allan, Billy Embleton, Laurie Mulrine, Robert Patterson, David Russon, Stephen McGahon, Richard Allen, John Carter and Keith Holt for their superb photographic contributions, without whom this book would not have been possible.

Finally, I would like to thank my Dad, John (Jack) Alexander MBE, for taking me as a small child to watch the trains at Central Station and Lamesley and Whitehill Point, and for instilling in me a lifelong interest in local history and railways.

Colin Alexander

It's not quite the 1970s, but the inclusion of this photograph is justified as it is so fascinating and I remember subsequently seeing this unique locomotive at Newcastle in the early 1970s. HS4000 *Kestrel* was a 4,000 hp prototype built by Hawker-Siddeley and is seen here leaving for King's Cross on 20 October 1969, flanked by a Class 25 and a 03 shunter. HS4000 was later exported to the USSR. (George Woods)

In complete contrast to the above, Eccles Colliery at Backworth was playing host in June 1971 to former Redheugh Gas Works 0-4-0ST, *Sir Cecil A. Cochrane,* for temporary storage. The two-road NCB shed stands behind the engine. The locomotive was eventually moved to the Tanfield Railway, where she survives in preservation. Industrial steam such as this is vivid in my childhood memory. (Billy Embleton)

Looking east from Newcastle's Castle Keep, built by the son of William the Conqueror on the site of Pons Aelius Roman fort on Hadrian's Wall, two-tone green Brush Type 4 No. 1999 approaches Central station with a train from Scotland. It is passing between a green English Electric Type 3 on a train of hoppers and a North Tyne loop DMU. (John Alexander)

In the early 1970s, containerisation in the shape of fast Freightliner trains was doing its bit to keep lorries off the roads. Tyneside had its own dedicated Freightliner terminal at Follingsby, on the Leamside line just south of Pelaw Junction. Gateshead's Brush Type 4 No. D1103, later No. 47520, stands alongside the yellow gantries on 28 July 1970. (Trevor Casey)

This 1970 shot is unusual as the photographer is also the driver of the train standing at Newcastle Central's platform 9. Gateshead driver and talented artist Albert Gilmour was rostered to drive the BR Sulzer Type 4 at the head of Liverpool-bound 1M67 as far as Leeds. Notice the short-lived Clayton Type 1, of which Gateshead had a small allocation, on the right. (Albert Gilmour)

Gateshead also had an allocation of BR Sulzer Type 2s, later Class 24, that were fitted with additional air hoses above the buffer beam to operate the doors on the hoppers of the Tyne Dock–Consett iron-ore trains. Two of them, No. D5110 and No. D5111, one in green and one in blue, though it is hard to tell, pass Newcastle Central on 13 February 1971. (Dave Jolly)

At the other end of Central station, English Electric Type 3 No. 6765, later No. 37065, rounds the curve off the King Edward VII Bridge with 6S41, a train of ICI tanks from Haverton Hill on Teesside to Leith on 8 April 1971. The reliable '37s' were the mainstay of freight on Tyneside for many years, this particular one enjoying a forty-five-year career. (Dave Jolly)

From a similar vantage point on the same day, English Electric Type 4 No. D213 *Andania* arrives at Newcastle with a train from Liverpool. It was a time of transition in liveries, the locomotive still wearing green with a small yellow warning panel, and one Mk I coach in the blue-and-grey rake still in maroon. Forth Goods Depot dominates the background. (Dave Jolly)

A stunning colour shot taken at Gateshead shed on 5 September 1971 with three BR Sulzer *Peaks*, an English Electric Type 3 and a Brush Type 4, with the old Greenesfield Works buildings on the right. No. D157, which would become No. 46020, was allocated to Bristol Bath Road at this time and looked a little shabby compared with her blue classmates. (Trevor Casey)

National Coal Board Austerity 0-6-0 STs No. 6 (built by Bagnall in 1944) and No. 49 (Robert Stephenson & Hawthorn 1943) stand in front of a coal conveyor at Backworth Colliery at Easter 1972. Nothing remains of this scene though happily both locomotives are preserved, No. 6 at the Caledonian Railway at Brechin and No. 49 at the Tanfield Railway, County Durham. (Laurie Mulrine)

It took a while for BR to repaint its diesel fleet from green into corporate blue, and this shot of Class 47s No. 1756 and No. 1990 at Gateshead on 5 May 1972 illustrates that point. No. 1756 was a Stratford engine, but No. 1990 is at her home depot. The locos were later renumbered No. 47162 and No. 47288 respectively. (Dave Jolly)

The flagships of BR's diesel fleet in the 1960s and 1970s were the English Electric Deltics. There were twenty-two of them and Gateshead had six, including No. 9014 *The Duke of Wellington's Regiment*, seen here at her home shed on 4 June 1972. At this time, the four-character train head-codes were in use, such as 1N08 here, indicating an express passenger train from King's Cross to the North Eastern Region. (Trevor Casey)

Another place where my Dad and I regularly watched the trains was next to the old cattle market that presented this view of the west end of Newcastle Central station, without having to splash out on a platform ticket! On 17 June 1972, preserved LNER A4 4-6-2 No. 4498 *Sir Nigel Gresley* makes a fine sight as she prepares to leave with the Steam Safari for Carlisle. (Dave Jolly)

The Steam Safari passes Forth Goods Yard behind No. 4498 *Sir Nigel Gresley* as she leaves Newcastle for Carlisle on 17 June 1972. Almost nothing remains of this scene today, although part of the Carlisle line remains as a headshunt for a small Engineer's Yard. On this very day, my Dad took me (aged eight) to see the A4 pass Haydon Bridge. (Dave Jolly)

Preston Division's Sulzer Type 2 No. 7547, later Class 25 No. 25197, whose two-tone green livery is broken by a blue panel covering the boiler grille, is seen leaving the King Edward VII Bridge with a local freight on 17 June 1972. The old Redheugh road bridge is in the background. This was replaced by a modern concrete viaduct in the early 1980s. (Dave Jolly)

Manors, east of Newcastle, had platforms for main line 'stoppers', and for Coast trains via the North Tyne loop that began and ended at Central, passing through Manors twice. Looking east in July 1972, we can see the line to Manors North in the foreground with the northbound main and Tynemouth lines curving to the right. There had previously been a freight curve connecting the two lines, joining New Bridge Street Goods Depot with the Quayside branch. (Geoff Allan)

Further east in July 1972 at Heaton Junction, the Tynemouth line is hemmed in by the old shed buildings on the north side, as English Electric Type 4, Class 40 No. 283 heads east, 'light engine'. The East Coast Main Line to Edinburgh is glimpsed through the gap to the left. I would occasionally see Class 40s on parcels trains at Tynemouth, although a '31' was more usual. (Geoff Allan)

First stop on the Tynemouth line east of Heaton Junction was Walkergate, which served the adjacent Parsons' Works. The Newcastle & North Shields Railway (N&NSR) opened this line in 1839 between Carliol Square and North Shields. This July 1972 shot shows the neglected, unwelcoming condition that was typical of our local stations at this time. No wonder Geordie commuters took to their Ford Cortinas. (Geoff Allan)

English Electric Type 4 No. 362, later No. 40162, looks superb at the head of a Freightliner train at Follingsby on 15 August 1972. No. 40162 was withdrawn in 1982 after a twenty-one-year career. The winding gear of Wardley Colliery can be seen on the left. At this time, similar structures could be seen all over North East England, and all were rail-connected. (Trevor Casey)

BR Sulzer Class 24 No. 5105, later No. 24105, stands at Tyne Yard on 12 September 1972. One of a batch built at Darlington Works, she was allocated to Gateshead shed from new in 1960, and was used on the Tyne Dock–Consett iron-ore trains. She lasted a mere fifteen years in service, spending her last months at Eastfield in Glasgow. (Laurie Mulrine)

Five years after steam was banished from BR, the National Coal Board was still making good use of its steam fleet. Around Backworth, there were several collieries and a railway network that led to a complex system of staithes on the Tyne at North Shields. Hunslet 1943-built Austerity 0-6-0ST No. 48 is busy with coal wagons at Backworth in 1973. She survives at the Strathspey Railway at Aviemore. (Billy Embleton)

Fenwick pit, east of Backworth, also in 1973 with NCB No. 16, built by Robert Stephenson & Hawthorn as late as 1957. I can remember tank engines like this shunting loaded coal wagons onto the staithes at Whitehill Point, next to what is now Royal Quays. Many of the buildings at Fenwick were finally demolished in 2016, leaving only the winding house. No. 16 is now at the Tanfield Railway. (Billy Embleton)

Preserved LNER B1 No. 1306 *Mayflower* and A3 No. 4472 *Flying Scotsman* are about to enter Bensham cutting with the North Eastern railtour from Liverpool Lime Street on 21 September 1975. This was a busy year for preservation in the North East, and we attended the 150th anniversary celebrations of the Stockton & Darlington Railway at Shildon. Note the derailed Presflo cement hopper on the left. (Dave Jolly)

The North Eastern again, leaving Newcastle Central behind B1 No. 1306 *Mayflower* and A4 No. 4472 *Flying Scotsman*. The train is crossing Forth Street with the return railtour to Liverpool Lime Street on 21 September 1975. A Sunbeam Rapier is parked below, while the Forth Ranks Engineers' Department is on the right, which is where I began my brief railway career in 1981. The innovative Centre for Life now stands on the site of Central Car Sales. (Dave Jolly)

To test and develop prototype Metrocars No. 4001 and No. 4002, the Tyne & Wear Passenger Transport Executive constructed a test track with a shed and level crossing beside Middle Engine Lane, North Shields. Inside the purpose-built shed, one of the prototypes is seen soon after delivery from Metro Cammell in 1975. Because my Dad worked for the PTE, I got to ride on and even drive the test trains. (John Alexander)

By the time the long hot summer of 1976 arrived, the Deltics had been in charge of the principal East Coast expresses for fifteen years. On 11 July, No. 55001 *St. Paddy* waits at platform 8 at Newcastle Central with 1S33, the 13.00 King's Cross–Aberdeen service. Sadly, along with No. 55020 *Nimbus*, she was one of the first two to be scrapped in 1980. (George Woods)

This one takes me back to my childhood, as I used to pass through Tynemouth station four times a day on my way to and from school (I always came home for dinner). On 19 August 1977, a Metro Cammell DMU is on its way around the North Tyne loop from Newcastle via Wallsend and Benton back to Newcastle again. There are two rakes of parcels vans in the south bay platforms. (Ernie Brack)

Tynemouth station was opened in 1882 by the North Eastern Railway (NER), and its footbridge had twin passageways, with a bridge between them for luggage barrows. There used to be barrow hoists at each end directly below the tangerine NE Region sign, which has the words 'Blyth & Newbiggin' painted over. This 19 August 1977 view shows the recently constructed wall that contained the parcels depot on the right. (Ernie Brack)

The 1.5 mile Metro test track ran from West Allotment as far as the A1058 Coast Road, on the route of an old mineral line. It incorporated sharp curves and steep inclines and even featured a Hornby trainset-style tunnel in the middle of a field! Prototype car No. 4002 is at the northern terminus, Murton Road, West Allotment on 24 June 1978. The end doors were not continued on the production batch. (Keith Holt)

Do you recognise yourself in this one? Some 1970s fashions are on display, including cagoules and parkas, on a summer Saturday at the west end of Newcastle Central, on 1 July 1978. I love this photograph as it sums up how I spent my days back then. The locomotives, incidentally, are No. 45129 on platform 9 and No. 47417 on platform 10. (Stephen McGahon)

English Electric Type 5 Deltic, No. 55022 *Royal Scots Grey* thunders through Heaton station with a southbound East Coast express in September 1978. Heaton Junction is beyond the second overbridge. North Tyne loop services stopped at the island platform here, but following closure in August 1980 the station was swept away, to be replaced by Byker Metro, about a quarter of a mile away. (Ernie Brack)

By September 1978, No. 283 has become No. 40083, and unusually for a Class 40, she is hauling a rake of Mk II air-conditioned stock as she passes through the cutting between the station and junction at Heaton to the carriage sidings. The station building spans the track in the distance. Beyond, the East Coast Main Line crosses the Ouseburn Viaduct into Manors then Newcastle Central. (Ernie Brack)

With Newcastle's St Nicholas Cathedral on the horizon, a very shiny No. 37141 descends the incline at Bensham in September 1978 with a train of bogie ballast hoppers. The East Coast Main Line is on the left, and the '37' could be heading for either Low Fell or Dunston and the Tyne Valley. (Ernie Brack)

The long bridge carrying Smithy Lane over the north end of Tyne Yard at Lamesley is somewhere else I would visit with my Dad, and one vivid memory is of a line of redundant Clayton Type 1 Class 17s dumped by the shed there in the early 1970s. They were long gone by 4 June 1979 when No. 37193 is in charge of a northbound cement train and a '31' heads a mixed freight. (Ernie Brack)

One of the larger stations on the North Tyne loop, Whitley Bay, was opened in 1910 to replace a smaller one in order to cope with growing crowds of holiday traffic, particularly from Glasgow during 'Fairs fortnight'. Special excursion trains were run in those long-gone, pre-Easyjet days. A DMU heads for West Monkseaton on 21 June 1979, three months before closure for conversion to Metro. (David Russon)

The Newcastle & Carlisle Railway was the first to reach across England from east to west and opened in 1838. A two-car DMU made up of a car each of Cravens and Metro Cammell types has stopped at Hexham with a Carlisle–Newcastle train around 1979. Such units were the mainstay of these services for three decades. (Ernie Brack)

English Electric Deltic No. 55007 *Pinza* accelerates towards 100 mph past Low Fell with a southbound train around 1980. The twin Napier-engined Type 5s were Britain's most powerful diesel locomotives, developing 3300 hp, and each member of the twenty-two-strong class notched up millions of miles in service on the East Coast Main Line. *Pinza* was one of the Finsbury Park allocation named after racehorses. (Ian Beattie)

A Scottish visitor stands beneath the massive signalling relay room at Newcastle Central in 1980. BRC&W Class 26 No. 26011 was built in 1959 as No. D5311, one of the Pilot Scheme locomotives ordered as part of BR's Modernisation Plan. The relay room contained hundreds of switches encased in glass boxes, which I helped replace in the early 1980s with newer, more compact versions. (Ian Beattie)

About 15 miles north of the Tyne, Ashington in Northumberland was still a thriving mining town in the early 1980s. No. 37078 is captured passing through the town's closed station on 8 February 1980. For a long time, there have been proposals to reopen the former Blyth & Tyne Railway from what is now Northumberland Park Metro north through Seaton Delaval to Bedlington and Ashington. (Dave Jolly)

No. 37078 again, this time in tandem with No. 37068 on a coal train on the King Edward VII Bridge over the Tyne, pursuing the tail end of an HST as it snakes into Newcastle Central station, which stretches across the background. Above the rear '37' is the former Stephenson Locomotive Works, where *Rocket* was built, and the new Metro Bridge completes the scene on 24 July 1980. (Dave Jolly)

A fine study of English Electric Class 40 No. 40078 taking water at Newcastle Central in 1980. She spent her entire twenty-one-year career allocated to Gateshead and York sheds. At this time, she was a regular performer on Newcastle–Edinburgh 'stoppers'. The 200-strong class gained a sizeable enthusiast following, like the Western diesel-hydraulics and Deltics. (Ian Beattie)

This desolate 1980 view by the Tyne at Gateshead is full of interest to the railway historian. The trackbed on the left is the route of the original Newcastle & Carlisle Railway that had its low-level terminus at Redheugh. The incline to the right connected it to the Brandling Junction Railway. The spindly Redheugh Bridge was dismantled a couple of years later. (Ernie Brack)

Preserved ex-LMSR Black 5 No. 4767 passes Gateshead East en route from Middlesbrough to Newcastle with The Northumbrian on 13 December 1980. I was on the train, and we had an eventful journey to Carlisle. No. 4767 failed near Greenhead, and we were propelled by No. 47280 as far as Low Row where No. 26034 was attached to drag us into Carlisle. No. 4767 was repaired though, and we continued via Settle to York. (Dave Jolly)

A classic Newcastle Central line-up in 1981 with a southbound HST, a Class 03 station pilot, No. 47523 with a northbound arrival and Metro Cammell DMUs for Sunderland in platforms 6 and 7. All of this is now history with the exceptions of the HST and the grand old station itself. No. 47523 was previously No. D1106 and was allocated to York at the time of the photograph. (Ian Robinson)

There were many industrial railways in the North East that operated ex-BR diesels, and the National Coal Board owned several. Former Class 08 No. D3088 had found a home at Bates Colliery in Blyth, Northumberland, where in 1981, she is in the company of a Barclay 0-6-0 diesel shunter. Bates was to last another five years. (Ian Robinson)

The substantial 1882 station at Tynemouth contained many offices and waiting rooms, as well as a newsagent on the concourse that served as a 'tuck shop' for the schools. At this time in 1981, the station was to be flattened and replaced by a minimalist Metro halt. In the end, the buildings were saved when the 'Friends of Tynemouth Station' pressurised the authorities. (Colin Alexander)

Gateshead in the early 1980s sees No. 37250 heading west with a train of loaded coal hoppers. The line that curves behind the Class 31 in the distance passes through the former Gateshead West station, forming part of the triangular junction at the south end of the High Level Bridge over the Tyne to Newcastle. (Ian Beattie)

Public services on the Metro commenced in August 1980 between Tynemouth and the new underground station at Haymarket. Meanwhile, construction of the bridge over the Tyne linking Central station and Gateshead meant that the service could be extended to Heworth the following year. There are, therefore, three rail bridges over the Tyne in the space of half a mile. A single Metrocar is on a test run in 1981, with the High Level Bridge beyond. (Colin Alexander)

In heavy snow, this early 1980s scene outside the main shed at Gateshead shows No. 40068 and No. 46027. Both of these Type 4s were 1950s designs with a 1Co-Co1 wheel arrangement derived from SR-designed prototypes Nos. 10201–10203. Their 130-plus tons of weight was spread across eight axles, two of which were unpowered. (Ian Beattie)

The early 1980s saw the first regular appearances of the new Class 56 freight locomotives in the region. The first thirty of the class were built in Romania, and it is one of these, No. 56020, that is seen in the snow at Gateshead. The depot would eventually receive its own allocation of the later Doncaster and Crewe-built locos. (Ian Beattie)

Before the NER opened its grand station at Tynemouth in 1882, both the N&NSR and Blyth & Tyne Railway had termini there. The N&NSR terminus boasted a handsome station building on Oxford Street, which remains to this day in residential use. It was built in 1847 when the 1839 line was extended through tunnels from North Shields. (Colin Alexander)

Tynemouth had two Blyth & Tyne termini, but little could be seen in my childhood other than the ruined coal drops at the original 1861 station. The Newcastle & North Shields station, however, still stood in 1981, having survived almost a hundred years as a goods yard after passenger closure in 1882. The large building was the station hotel. Coal trains used the sidings here until the late 1970s, usually hauled by Class 31s or 37s. Many years earlier, there was a railway from here down an incline to the North Pier. (Colin Alexander)

When the King Edward VII Bridge opened in 1906, it provided a unique circular flexibility to the rail layout of Newcastle and Gateshead. In this 1981 scene, No. 55022 *Royal Scots Grey* has crossed the Tyne and is heading for the south. On 2 January 1982, she hauled the Deltic Scotsman Farewell railtour from Edinburgh to King's Cross to bring about the end of an era. (Ian Beattie)

Deltic No. 55017 *The Durham Light Infantry* moves onto the 'ash-heaps' at Gateshead shed in 1981. Part of the breakdown train is seen on the left, and the pale brickwork on the depot building marks the section that was rebuilt following tunnelling work during construction of the Metro below. Within a year, all of the Deltics were withdrawn from service. (Ian Robinson)

The junction station at Manors replaced the Blyth & Tyne Railway's New Bridge Street and the N&NSR's Carliol Square, both of which were terminus stations. No. 45074 heads for Heaton through Manors station on 14 February 1981, with the closed Manors North in the background. (Dave Jolly)

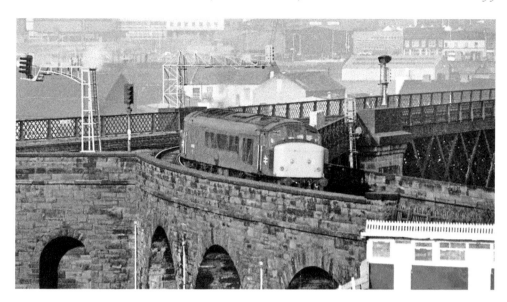

The telephoto lens accentuates the sharp curve at King Edward VII Bridge Junction as No. 45033 is about to cross the Tyne from Gateshead shed to Newcastle, presumably on her way to collect empty coaching stock from Heaton, on 14 February 1981. The allotment in the foreground is home to a typical Geordie pigeon 'cree'. (Dave Jolly)

The North East area of the NCB had a fleet of Class 14, 650 hp diesel-hydraulics that were only about four years old when declared surplus by BR in 1968. My first encounter with them was at Weetslade in February 1981 where NCB staff allowed us to ride in the cab of No. D9504, seen here as NCB 506. Bizarrely, this locomotive was later used in the Channel Tunnel construction and is now preserved. (Colin Alexander)

By 14 March 1981, which was my seventeenth birthday, the Deltics were drawing the crowds on station platforms up and down the country, and Newcastle was no exception. Everyone knew the end was drawing near for the class, but No. 55013 *The Black Watch* was still going strong, seen here on 1S12, the 05.50 King's Cross–Aberdeen, which she worked as far as Edinburgh. (Colin Alexander)

Having been diverted off the main line at Benton Junction, No. 40159 takes 1S14, the 08.10 Newcastle–Edinburgh train around the curve towards the future site of Palmersville Metro station, as she heads for the former Blyth & Tyne line to eventually reach Morpeth, on 13 April 1981. She is about to pass another Class 40 on a parcels train and the eagle-eyed among you will spot a Metrocar above the leading parcels vans. (Ian Beattie)

On 7 May 1981, a Cravens Class 105 DMU is under the roof at South Shields station. This would close a few weeks later, eventually to be replaced by the new Metro station closer to the main street. The station was opened by the NER in 1879, and the line was electrified in 1938, thirty-four years after the North Tyne loop. (Colin Alexander)

A Newcastle–Middlesbrough train composed of a two-car Cravens Class 105 DMU led by driving trailer No. E56425 leaves the High Level Bridge and prepares to stop at Gateshead East on 6 June 1981. The floodlight just visible top left was at St James' Park, with the angled roof of the East Stand to its right. This stand was dwarfed by later development of the stadium. (George Woods)

By 6 June 1981, when No. E43058 is seen taking the Gateshead West curve off the High Level Bridge, the Inter-City 125 HST fleet had taken almost all of the principal main line workings away from the Deltics. I wonder if Robert Stephenson could have visualised 125 mph-capable trains crossing his bridge during its construction in the 1840s? (George Woods)

Travelling towards Carlisle along the Tyne Valley line, one of the many rural stations is Stocksfield, where a Hexham–Newcastle Metro Cammell DMU is seen departing on 6 June 1981. The leading car carries the short-lived 'refurbished' livery of near white with a blue stripe, whereas the other three cars are wearing the later blue and grey. (Ernie Brack)

Newcastle's medieval Castle Keep provides a dizzying viewpoint over both the High Level Bridge and Central station. No. 31222 brings a short passenger train over from Gateshead on 6 June 1981, with the buildings of the former Greenesfield Works to the right, concealing Gateshead shed. Top left is the famous *Get Carter* multi-storey car park, now demolished. (George Woods)

A Carlisle-bound hybrid DMU, composed of a Class 105 car built by Cravens and three Class 101 Metro Cammell cars, leaves Newcastle Central and passes Forth Junction, with the remains of Forth Goods on the right and the Tyne Bridge visible in the distance. A hopper wagon on the coal drops to the left completes the scene, taken on 6 June 1981. (George Woods)

A low-angle shot that accentuates the 100-ton bulk of a Deltic, as No. 55011 *The Royal Northumberland Fusiliers* sets off from platform 8 at Central station on 20 June 1981 with 1V93, the Edinburgh–Plymouth service, which was by this time a typical Deltic working as far as York, having been 'cascaded' from top-link duties by the arrival of the HSTs. (Colin Alexander)

It is the dawning of a new era at Newcastle on 22 June 1981 as prototype railbus No. 140001 enters the east end of Central station. By now, most of the DMU fleet was more than twenty years old, and these four-wheeled vehicles would prove to be an economic, if not an ergonomic replacement. Basically a bus body on a freight van chassis, it would win no awards for its aesthetics either. (Colin Alexander)

Recently reallocated from Lincoln to Gateshead, shunter No. 03021 is on duty in Newcastle Central's 'wallside' on 25 July 1981 as No. 31171 arrives at platform 10 with a summer-only service from Filey. Other destinations served by such seasonal trains to and from Newcastle were Yarmouth and Scarborough. They gave enthusiasts the opportunity to travel on relatively rare motive power. (Colin Alexander)

Fresh from overhaul at Doncaster Works in July 1981, English Electric Class 50 No. 50040 *Leviathan* hauls the test train past the outside of Newcastle Central. She has taken advantage of the circular layout between Gateshead and Newcastle to turn around before heading south. Note the signalling relay room projecting through the station's curtain wall, and the NER water tower on the right. (Ian Beattie)

By the summer of 1981, Deltic No. 55015 *Tulyar* had lost her trademark Finsbury Park white cabs, although she would regain them later in the year for some of the final railtours. Here, one of her twin Napier engines is being started up in characteristically smoky fashion in Newcastle Central's platform 4 as she prepares to depart with 1S08, the 07.05 'stopper' to Edinburgh. (Neil Jordan)

By the time the first 125 Class 40s were in service, the old folding disc indicators were redundant, and BR was using four-character head-codes on its diesel and electric locomotives. The end communication doors, however, were still wanted, so several loco types had split head-code boxes, as seen here on No. 40138 with an ICI tanker train at Newcastle in 1981. (Ian Beattie)

Outside South Gosforth shed around 1981 is one of the five Metro Works locomotives, WL3, ordered from Brush in the late 1970s. All five were sold in 1991 to the Channel Tunnel construction company. They were replaced by smaller battery-electric locomotives, and at least one of the WLs is preserved. Metrocar No. 4007 looks smart in the original yellow-and-white PTE livery. (Neil Jordan)

Beyond Heaton Junction, the main line curves north and crosses the A1058 Coast Road on a skew bridge beside the former Wills cigarette factory, seen in the background here. This art deco structure is now luxury flats. Deltic No. 55009 *Alycidon* is gathering speed as she passes a NER milepost and heads for Edinburgh in 1981, probably on 1S76, the 09.40 from King's Cross. (Neil Jordan)

Alycidon again, this time at Gateshead shed, also in 1981. In one of the flats in the background, the characters played by Michael Caine and Britt Ekland enjoyed an intimate scene in the iconic film *Get Carter*. The flats, like Gateshead shed, are history. *Alycidon* meanwhile is a regular performer on the main line today thanks to the Deltic Preservation Society. (Ian Beattie)

By 31 October 1981 when this photograph was taken, the remaining Deltics were in demand for enthusiasts' specials and had just nine weeks left. No. 55002 *The King's Own Yorkshire Light Infantry* is captured wearing an approximation of her original livery as applied by the National Railway Museum, who were to become her custodians. She is leaving Newcastle with The Celtic Deltic for Edinburgh. (Ian Beattie)

Christmas Eve 1981 was bleak in every respect for Deltic followers. With one week to go until she had the dubious honour of working the last ever Deltic-hauled BR service train, No. 55017 *The Durham Light Infantry* stands proudly alongside one of her successors. She is on 1S12, the 05.50 King's Cross to Aberdeen. (Colin Alexander)

Also in December 1981, No. 40049 has a more mundane task as she heads a northbound mixed freight of a type that has long since disappeared, past a snowy Newcastle Central. She was delivered from Vulcan Foundry new to Gateshead as No. D249 in 1959 and spent time at various depots across the North, ending her days as a York engine. (Ian Beattie)

For a long time, the fifty-six members of Class 46 were divided equally between Laira shed in Plymouth and Gateshead. This reflected their chief sphere of operation, which was passenger services between the North East and the South West. Gateshead's No. 46039 is probably on such a working in the Newcastle snow of December 1981. (Ian Beattie)

No. 47401 started life as No. D1500, the first of the class of 512 Brush Type 4s. In December 1981, she had recently been given the name *North Eastern*, and she still looks immaculate from that ceremony as she stands at Newcastle's platform 8. She is now preserved at the Midland Railway Centre at Butterley. (Ian Beattie)

The freezing weather did not deter the crowds lining the 393-mile route of the Deltic Scotsman Farewell on 2 January 1982. No. 55015 *Tulyar* hauled the northbound leg from King's Cross to Edinburgh, and No. 55022 *Royal Scots Grey* performed the return journey that evening. It was the end of an era, and we would not hear that Napier sound on the main line again until 1996 when the first preservation-era Deltic railtour was run. (Neil Jordan)

By the mid-1970s, pretty much anything that moved on BR was painted blue. Class 40 No. 40106 had achieved celebrity status by retaining her green livery; in fact, she had it re-applied in 1978, and here she is at platform 9 of Newcastle Central with 1Z09, a return excursion from Edinburgh Waverley to Manchester Victoria on 27 February 1982. She is one of seven Class 40s in preservation. (Dave Jolly)

A westbound Freightliner train from Follingsby, hauled by No. 45052, passes the recently opened Metro station at Gateshead Stadium on 22 April 1982. The Metro service to Heworth had begun in 1981, then was extended to South Shields in 1984. The track on the left leads into the Tyneside Central Freight Depot. (Dave Jolly)

No. 37094 approaches Carr House with a scrap train from the demolished Consett steelworks on 11 May 1982, on the 1 in 55 climb from Low Yard to the summit 880 feet above sea level. Above the train is the remains of the iron-ore wagon tippler and the unusual Consett Fell signal box, built by the Consett Iron Company but operated by BR. The scene today shows little evidence of the railway's existence. The only remaining features are the houses on the left and the locomotive, which survives as DRS No. 37716. (Stephen McGahon)

At Ashington Colliery on 1 July 1982, Gateshead's No. 37250 is seen alongside the former BR No. D9521, now numbered 9312/90 and looking immaculate in her recently applied NCB blue-and-red livery. Note the variety of coal wagons and the vast NCB engineering workshops in the background. Ashington was known as the 'world's largest coal-mining village'. It is hard to believe that all of this is history. Both locos survive though, No. 37250 at the Eden Valley Railway and No. D9521 at Llangollen. (Colin Alexander)

While the collieries north of the Tyne relied on steam power, the Harton Coal Company in South Shields boasted an electric railway, dating from the 1900s. In 1982, it was possible to see an operational fleet of fascinating electric locomotives, some dating back to the Edwardian era. This is NCB No. 11, built by English Electric in the 1950s, with the substantial Westoe colliery buildings behind. (Colin Alexander)

The electric locomotives solved the operational problems posed by low-roofed tunnels and tight curves on the route to the staithes at South Shields. NCB No. 9 is seen here at Westoe in 1982 as she approached the age of seventy. She was built by AEG in Germany the year before the First World War broke out, and is now retired at the Tanfield Railway, along with E10. No. 2 meanwhile is at Beamish Museum. (Colin Alexander)

An unidentified Class 47 hauls a Carlisle–Newcastle service past Scotswood signal box around 1982, shortly before the line closed and services were diverted via the King Edward VII Bridge and Dunston. Scotswood box controlled the junction for the former North Wylam line, the last vestige of which is on the right. The cooling towers of Stella North power station dominate the background. Signal box, railway and power station are all history. (Craig Oliphant)

Heaton Junction was an important location east of Newcastle, where the Tynemouth branch and the main line to Edinburgh diverged. In between the two lines, on the site of the former Heaton steam shed were carriage sidings. In August 1982, we see No. 40047 on the main line with a ballast train passing a sister locomotive on her way into the sidings. These lineside shots were achievable because the photographer was a BR employee at the time. (David Tweddle)

Another unusual photo that was only obtainable with a BR permit and a hi-vis vest, No. 46016 awaits departure from Newcastle Central's platform 10 in September 1982. New to Derby as No. D153 in 1962, reallocations over the years saw her based at sheds in England, Scotland and Wales, including Haymarket, Gateshead, Cardiff and Laira. She was withdrawn in 1983. (David Tweddle)

Sulzer Type 4s to the fore as No. 45033 heads towards Newcastle on 15 October 1982 with a parcels train past Tyneside Central Freight Depot, which opened in 1963 just east of Gateshead, close to the site of the former Borough Gardens steam shed. In the background, No. 47429 waits to leave with 6M66, the 16.05 Speedlink to Willesden. (Dave Jolly)

Stella South power station was west of Blaydon, across the Tyne from Stella North. On 26 October 1982, No. 37161 and No. 37193 double-head a Workington to Lackenby steel train past sister No. 37030, dwarfed by the giant lighting towers. A CEGB diesel shunter may be glimpsed. Both of the Stella power stations closed in 1991, but No. 37030 soldiered on until 1999 as No. 37701. No. 37161 meanwhile ended her days in Spain as No. 37899, and No. 37193 was scrapped in 2008 as No. 37375. (Craig Oliphant)

Class 56 No. 56075, built at Doncaster in 1980, is captured at Stella North power station, near Newburn on the north bank of the Tyne west of Newcastle, on 11 November 1982. This was served by the stub of the old North Wylam route that deviated from the Newcastle to Carlisle line at Scotswood and re-joined it just west of Wylam, passing the cottage where George Stephenson was born. In the background, the distinctive cone of Lemington bottle works can be seen. (Craig Oliphant)

The former Blyth & Tyne Railway is used as a diversionary route when engineering work takes place, and at Bedlington an HST is seen rounding the curve from the Morpeth direction, around 1982. To the right is the line towards Cambois and Ashington. Remarkably much of Bedlington station stands today, despite losing its passenger service in 1964. (Craig Oliphant)

The last vacuum-braked-only Class 40 in service was No. 40009, formerly No. D209, last of the original Pilot Scheme batch built in 1958. She is seen here approaching Manors with a parcels train sometime around 1982, below the buildings of New Bridge Street. The tunnel on the right once led to the steep and tightly curved Quayside branch, on which the NER used a pair of electric locomotives. One of these is preserved in the National Collection. (Ian Beattie)

When the Metro system took over the route of the former NER Ponteland branch to Bank Foot, BR freight trains serving the Rowntree factory at Fawdon had to share the track with the Supertrams. This arrangement continued until the late 1980s, when like most local freight workings in the area it ceased to exist. In this shot taken around 1984, No. 31290 propels a train of vans into the factory sidings. The Metro line has since been extended to the Airport. (Craig Oliphant)

The driver of this Class 45/1 is applying the power as she accelerates around the banked curve out of Bensham cutting and heads south, around 1982. The train has just crossed the bridge that carries the main line over the route to Norwood Junction for either Blaydon or Low Fell. The distinctive terraced houses on the right have since been demolished. (Ian Beattie)

On the south bank of the Tyne between Gateshead and Dunston on the remaining stub of the old Redheugh branch, No. 03078 and her match truck are seen shunting pick-up goods at a riverside scrapyard around 1983. Dunston power station is in the background. Needless to say this area is unrecognisable today. Happily, No. 03078 survives in preservation at the Stephenson Railway Museum. (Craig Oliphant)

The 'Riverside' branch deviated from the Tynemouth line at Byker and followed the north bank of the Tyne as far as Percy Main, serving the shipyards. It lost its passenger service in 1973, but in truncated form, it continued to see freight traffic into the late 1980s. No. 31169 is seen shunting at Wallsend's famous Swan Hunter shipyard around 1984. Beyond the buildings on the right is the site of the Roman fort of Segedunum. (Craig Oliphant)

Newcastle's overall roof looks even more striking when illuminated at night, as seen in this excellent time-exposure shot in 1982. The station roof is now sensitively and beautifully restored, one of the city's many architectural gems. The locomotive is a Class 45/1, one of fifty of the class of 127 that were fitted with electric train heating, and which were mostly used on the Midland main line. (Ian Beattie)

Another night shot in 1982 showing one of Newcastle's ubiquitous 204 hp Class 03 station pilots, No. 03063 shunting parcels vans in platform 12. These shunters were always coupled to an old 'Conflat' wagon because the locomotive's short wheelbase would not reliably trip the track circuit, an essential part of the railway signalling system at the time. (Ian Beattie)

A National Coal Board Hunslet 0-6-0 diesel hauls coal to the Derwenthaugh Coke Works with a shunter riding on the footsteps, on 11 November 1982, four years before closure. This was until the late 1960s the home of A No. 5, seen later in the book. Driving along the A694 today, seen in the left of the picture, you would have no clue that any of this industry existed. (Craig Oliphant)

The Stourton Saloon was a former Gloucester Railway Carriage & Wagon Co. Class 100 DMU, formerly Nos SC51122 and SC56300, converted for use as the Eastern Region inspection saloon and renumbered DB975664 and DB975637. It is seen here during a visit to the coal staithes at Cambois, North Blyth around 1984. (Craig Oliphant)

No. 40197 was one of the last Class 40s to enter service, as No. D397 in 1962. She is passing Washington signal box with a parcels train on the single-track Leamside line around 1982. In August 1980, I was on an overnight train from King's Cross to Edinburgh behind sister loco No. 40103 and was diverted via the Leamside and the Blyth & Tyne, the only time I ever travelled on those routes. (Ian Beattie)

In teeming rain, and seen from the shelter of part of the old Greenesfield Works building at Gateshead are No. 40003, No. 31256 and a Class 37. No. 40003 was once No. D203, one of the original batch of ten Pilot Scheme Class 40s. She entered service in 1958 and was withdrawn later in the same year that the photograph was taken, 1982. (Colin Alexander)

Also taken around 1982, a Hexham-bound Class 101 DMU is seen at Scotswood Junction, with the truncated North Wylam branch to the left serving Stella North power station. Scotswood station stood on this site with two platforms on each line. The Vickers-Armstrong factory that manufactured armaments is on the right, beside the famous Scotswood Road. (Craig Oliphant)

For many years, Gateshead had a large allocation of Class 46s, but by late 1982, No. 46050 was withdrawn and dumped on the 'ash-heaps', at the end of her twenty-year career. She has evidently suffered some vandalism to her cab windows, and it would be 1985 before she was scrapped at Swindon Works. The Queen Elizabeth II Metro Bridge over the Tyne can be glimpsed on the left. (Ian Beattie)

Many of the Class 46s soldiered on beyond the end of 1982, and here we see No. 46017 bringing a train of empty Mk II coaching stock into the carriage sidings at Heaton Junction. The long roof of the Chillingham Arms dominates the skyline above the locomotive. The last of the class was withdrawn in November 1984. (David Tweddle)

The importance of Manors station gradually diminished through the 1970s. We used to occasionally board a Deltic-hauled Edinburgh 'stopper' at the Central and get off again at Manors, carrying a Tyne & Wear Travel card. Not strictly valid, but it was the nearest we got to being rebellious teenagers. By 1983, only the main line island platform remained in use, the rest falling derelict. (Colin Alexander)

A Class 45/1 threads her way along the viaduct between Manors and Newcastle Central in March 1983 with what is probably a Liverpool train. She is about to pass between the Castle Keep and the Black Gate, which were forever separated when the Newcastle & Berwick Railway drove its route right through the castle that gave the city its name in 1080, having previously been called Monkchester. (David Tweddle)

An unusual shot showing a maintenance worker's view of the east-end bay platforms at Newcastle Central in March 1983. Once the Metro was in operation beneath Newcastle city centre, most of the bays were redundant and were to become a car park. The platform on the far right was designated the parcels bay. That with the yellow Leyland Sherpa van on it was platform 1. The roof over these platforms is a remnant of one that once extended across the whole site. (David Tweddle)

Celebrity green '40' No. 40106 poses on the freight lines beside Newcastle Central in March 1983. She is preserved at the Nene Valley Railway near Peterborough. Several of the earlier Class 40s were named after ocean liners, and the preserved No. 40106 now carries *Atlantic Conveyor* nameplates in the same style, commemorating the vessel lost in the Falklands conflict. (David Tweddle)

The 1882 NER station at Tynemouth joined the former Blyth & Tyne with the Newcastle & North Shields route to form the North Tyne loop. In 1983, with the advent of the Metro, it seemed likely that this great Victorian station would be demolished, so I took some monochrome pictures for posterity. A kit of parts for an intended new footbridge can be seen on the left. Fortunately, a reprieve was won, and the restored station looks stunning today. (Colin Alexander)

A typical scene at the east end of Gateshead shed in May 1983, with some of the original Greenesfield Works buildings in the background. No. 37237 of Eastfield is seen with an earlier sister engine. Detail differences can be seen: '237' has a centre head-code, now blanked over, and some of the fairing around the buffers has been cut away. Her sister is the original split-box type that accommodated the little-used end communication doors. (David Tweddle)

On 18 May 1983, No. 47580 *County of Essex* was assigned to Royal Train duty, when Princess Diana visited Newcastle for the official opening of the new Redheugh road bridge. A Class 45 is alongside. No. 47580 entered service in 1964 as No. D1762, becoming No. 47167 in 1973, and then No. 47580 when fitted with electric train-heating equipment. She is still operational on the main line with West Coast Rail in 2016. (Colin Alexander)

The year 1983 was a time of transition in the haulage of North East freight traffic, as the new Class 56s were beginning to take over what was previously the preserve of the Class 37s. The stabling point at Cambois (pronounced 'Cammus') is playing host to examples of both in this shot. Over 300 Class 37s were built by English Electric and many are still in service today. The North Sea is on the right with the seaside village of Newbiggin on the horizon. (Neil Jordan)

A pair of Class 56s led by No. 56076 *Blyth Power* run past the NER signal box at Holywell, sometime around 1983. This is on the former Blyth & Tyne Railway route, and the locomotives are travelling from Blyth. They will shortly take the curve westwards to bring them alongside the Metro formation until they join the main line at Benton Junction. The line remains in use, albeit as a single track, but the signal box is long gone. (Neil Jordan)

A Class 45 hauls the Redbank parcels train out of the sidings at Heaton Junction around 1983. The new Chillingham Road Metro station is on the far right, occupying the formation of the Tynemouth branch, and the East Coast Main Line curves away to the north. Another Class 45 is on a rake of air-conditioned Mk IIs awaiting departure for Newcastle. (Craig Oliphant)

A classic nocturnal shot of Newcastle station pilot No. 03063 and her match truck at the west end of the 'wallside' sidings in 1983. She was one of the dual-braked examples, having the air reservoirs in front of the cab. Built as D2063 in 1959, she spent her working life in Yorkshire until she was transferred to Gateshead in 1982. She survives in preservation at the North Norfolk Railway. (Ian Beattie)

By 1983, Ashington's No. 9312/90 looks somewhat less immaculate than when we saw her last. Major overhauls of these locomotives were carried out at the NCB's Philadelphia workshops in County Durham. I once saw one on a low-loader crossing the A1058 Coast Road in Newcastle, presumably en route there from the Northumberland coalfield. (David Tweddle)

No. 40118, one of the batch of twenty built by Robert Stephenson & Hawthorn at Darlington, arrives at Newcastle in 1983. She gave twenty-five years of service to BR, ending her days renumbered No. 97408 when used in Crewe remodelling work, before being withdrawn in 1986. She is currently undergoing restoration at the Birmingham Railway Museum, Tyseley. (Colin Alexander)

Also at Newcastle, a pair of Class 20s, No. 20218 and No. 20221, pass with a train of cement wagons on 22 July 1983. These English Electric Type 1s were infrequent visitors to Tyneside. This pair is from the later batch of 100 built in the late 1960s to replace the disastrously unreliable Clayton Class 17s. (Dave Jolly)

Glimpsed through the steelwork of a gantry at Newcastle in 1983 is No. 37078 again, and this time she is on empty coaching stock on the freight-avoiding lines. Sometimes, to temporarily free up one of the three through platforms, an empty train would cross one of the bridges to Gateshead then return by the other one. Since remodelling, Newcastle now has five through platforms. (Colin Alexander)

Until 1982, Carlisle-bound trains travelled along the north bank of the Tyne through Elswick and Scotswood, then crossed the river to Blaydon. By 1983, when No. 40135 was pictured at Elswick, the line was truncated and was freight-only. The locomotive has lost the water tank from between her bogies as she no longer has a train-heating boiler. No. 40135 is now preserved as No. D335 at the East Lancashire Railway, which is a magnet for heritage diesel enthusiasts. (Colin Alexander)

Looking north from Smithy Lane Bridge at Lamesley, No. 47372 speeds south past Tyne Yard on 27 September 1983. Compare the freight stock to that seen a decade earlier, much of which belonged in the steam age. The new A1 Western Bypass crosses the main line just beyond the back of the train. (Dave Jolly)

An unidentified Class 40 of the batch numbered Nos 40151–40199 hauls a tanker train through platform 8 at Newcastle, around 1983. Fewer than twenty of this popular class of 200 would last into 1985. They will be remembered for their distinctive whistling sound, and seven are preserved for posterity, including 1958-built pioneer No. D200. (Colin Alexander)

I did not take many pictures of Inter-City 125 High Speed Trains, as they had replaced my beloved Deltics, but even I would have to admit that they have been one of the most successful designs to run on Britain's rails. This is power car No. 43192, seen around 1983 at Newcastle. Although many have been re-engined, the fleet is still going strong, the first having entered service in 1976. (Colin Alexander)

Contrasting visions of the future at Newcastle. One day around 1983, I heard the familiar throaty sound of a pair of Class 37s. Expecting to see the usual rake of hopper wagons behind them, imagine my surprise when the payload turned out to be prototype Advanced Passenger Train No. 370007. I believe that the APT-P was undergoing brake tests at night on the 'racing stretch' south of Northallerton. The convoy is on its way to Heaton depot alongside a departing HST. (Colin Alexander)

The depot at the former Metro test track on Middle Engine Lane in North Shields had by the early 1980s become the fledgling Stephenson Railway Museum. George Stephenson's *Billy* of 1826 is possibly the fifth-oldest surviving locomotive in the world, and once ran on what is now the Bowes Railway in Springwell. For many years, she stood on a plinth at the end of the High Level Bridge. (Colin Alexander)

Another unique exhibit at Middle Engine Lane is NER electric motor luggage van No. 3267, seen here around 1983 with restoration under way. She is one of two surviving vehicles from the NER's pioneering Tyneside electrification scheme of 1904, the other being Quayside shunter No. 1 at Locomotion, Shildon. The electric passenger service ended on North Tyneside in 1967 to be replaced by DMUs. (Colin Alexander)

The Consett Iron Company used a Stephenson 'long-boiler' design of 0-6-0 pannier tank, and the sole surviving example is preserved at the Stephenson Railway Museum. She was employed at Derwenthaugh Coke Works until the 1960s. I was a volunteer at the museum and was involved in her restoration to steam. Kitson-built A No. 5 of 1883 is on a demonstration freight near Percy Main in the 1980s. (Richard Vogel)

Staying with the Consett theme, there was a farewell railtour to the former steel town following the demise of the steelworks and before closure of the line. No. 46026 *Leicestershire and Derbyshire Yeomanry*, the only named Class 46, is at South Pelaw on 17 March 1984. She is carrying the smoke box number-plate from No. 92066, one of the 9F 2-10-0s allocated to the Tyne Dock–Consett iron-ore trains until the 1960s. (Dave Jolly)

No. 46026 seen later in 1984 at Newcastle, having lost her nameplates. By the end of the year, she was withdrawn from service. Here she is on either 1V50 or 1A40, which were the Royal Mail travelling post office trains for Bristol and London, respectively. Later in the 1980s, I worked 12-hour nightshifts in the sorting rooms underneath the station in the run-up to Christmas. Trains would unload bags of mail that descended into the bowels of the station, and their contents had to be sorted by destination. (Ian Beattie)

Tyne Yard opened in 1963 and was a busy location while there was freight traffic on Tyneside. BR Sulzer No. 25034 of Eastfield shed, Glasgow, is moving off the yard 'light engine' having brought in a freight from Carlisle, around 1984. Note the variety of wagons in the sidings, including many for permanent way work. The yard is nowadays a shadow of its former self. (Robert Patterson)

Looking north from Park Lane Bridge on the eastern edge of Gateshead towards Newcastle, No. 37250 hauls a ballast train towards Pelaw on 30 March 1984. The line beyond the brake van curves left to High Street Junction where trains can be routed through either Gateshead East station onto the High Level Bridge over the Tyne to Newcastle, or west, past Gateshead depot. (Dave Jolly)

Haltwhistle, about 45 miles west of Tynemouth, is the point where the rail network parts company from the River Tyne, or more precisely, the South Tyne. The Tyne proper is formed where the North and South Tyne meet near Border Counties Junction. Viewed from Haltwhistle signal box, a Class 47 heads a Carlisle-bound train past the stub of the former Alston branch in April 1984. (Colin Alexander)

The westbound island platform at Haltwhistle was staggered from the eastbound platform. No. 40056 had failed here on 13 April 1984 on a Mossend to Harwich freight and was waiting to be removed a few days later. She was condemned in September of that year. A Class 31 passes 'light engine' heading for Newcastle. (Colin Alexander)

The market town of Hexham in the Tyne Valley is the principal station between Carlisle and Newcastle, and in April 1984, it still boasted an operational goods yard. Brush Type 2 No. 31271 is seen shunting Ciba-Geigy epoxy resin tank wagons beside the NER goods shed. This traffic supplied the nearby chipboard factory, but sadly, it ceased in the early 1990s. (Colin Alexander)

Alongside the River Tyne at Blaydon on 7 April 1984, pioneer Class 40 No. 40122/D200 with green livery restored is in charge of 1Z69 the Knotty Circular Rambler that has travelled from Stafford to Carlisle and will return via Newcastle and Leeds. In the background is Stella North power station. Blaydon once boasted an engine shed, code 52C, with an allocation of a hundred locomotives in 1948. (Dave Jolly)

In May 1969, an Aberdeen 'sleeper' hauled by Deltic No. 9011 derailed at speed on the notorious Morpeth curve, north of Newcastle. History repeated itself on 24 June 1984 when No. 47452 on the 19.50 King's Cross to Aberdeen came off at the same location. There were no fatalities, amazingly, which was testimony to the rigidity of the Mk III sleeping cars. Two days later, No. 25154 is in attendance with the Kingmoor breakdown train. (Craig Oliphant)

Platforms 11–15 at the west end of Newcastle Central were used mainly for Hexham and Carlisle services, and for parcels trains. On 19 July 1984, No. 40155 is seen in platform 12 with 1V97, the 16.02 parcels train for Bristol, having received some cosmetic attention, presumably from working a railtour. She was withdrawn six months later in January 1985. (Colin Alexander)

A Class 101 DMU pauses at Hexham's neat station beneath a clear blue sky on 20 August 1984. The Tyne Valley line is not a fast route and even now, Northern Rail's fastest Newcastle–Carlisle service takes 82 minutes for the 60-mile journey between the two cities. Hexham is well worth a visit with its Abbey founded in Saxon times, medieval Moot Hall and Old Gaol. (George Woods)

Another typical NER structure at Hexham is the Grade II listed gantry signal box. They used to be all over the system, but Hexham's is one of the few that remain today. On 20 August 1984, a Metro Cammell Class 101 DMU, carrying the Tyne & Wear PTE logo, sets off for Newcastle. (George Woods)

Three of the famous bridges that link Newcastle and Gateshead are seen in this 1984 shot of a Metro Cammell DMU crossing Stephenson's ingenious double-decked High Level Bridge of 1849. Armstrong's 1876 Swing Bridge is below with the iconic 1928 Tyne Bridge beyond. Scaffolding is in place on the latter for the repaint that restored its original green colour scheme. (Colin Alexander)

Speaking of original green colour schemes, miraculously, Swindon-built ex-BR Class 14 No. D9502 retained her original 1964 livery right until the end of her NCB career at Ashington twenty years later. I first encountered No. D9502 in this condition at Weetslade in 1982, and when I last saw her at Peak Rail, Derbyshire, in 2009, she had still managed to avoid the paintbrush! (Ian Robinson)

On a rare bright day in Cambois, BR 350 hp shunter No. 08872 is busy with 'merry-go-round' hoppers, sometime in 1985. Although all of this scene is now gone, beyond the school and the houses to the left there remains a railway where in a complete reversal of centuries of tradition, imported coal is transferred from ship to train and taken to the power station at Lynemouth. (Ernie Brack)

No. 56079 is dwarfed by the chimneys of Blyth 'B' power station on 4 August 1985. The '56' is drawing its train of 'merry-go-round' hoppers slowly through the unloading shed. I was fortunate enough to be given a guided tour of the power station at around this time, thanks to the father of a friend of mine. A landmark that could be seen from miles away, Blyth power station was demolished in 2003. (Dave Jolly)

No. 37226 has precious cargo in tow as she hauls preserved Deltic No. 9000 *Royal Scots Grey* past Low Fell as part of 6E61 Speedlink from Mossend Yard to Healey Mills on 6 September 1985. The Deltic had been on display at an open day at her former depot at Haymarket a couple of weeks earlier. (Dave Jolly)

By the mid-1980s, the railway began to brighten up its drab corporate blue image, and many locomotives were repainted with wraparound yellow cabs, black window surrounds and light grey roofs, along with large logos and numbers. No. 56095 is seen at Tyne Yard on 'merry-go-round' empties on 27 September 1985. The tall mast in the centre of the shot was part of the microwave radio link between Newcastle, Darlington and York. (Dave Jolly)

A little further south, the formation of the Consett branch is seen curving away to the left as No. 47351 passes Ouston Junction with 1M19, the 17.50 Newcastle–Liverpool Lime Street service on 27 September 1985. The bridge on the right once carried the Stanhope & Tyne Railway towards Tyne Dock. (Dave Jolly)

Much of Ashington's coal output was taken by train to feed Blyth power station, which was served by the railway complex at Cambois, once the location of North Blyth steam shed. The four chimneys of the power station form the background to this mid-1980s shot of No. 56130, built at Crewe in 1983, and whose new livery is already filthy! (Ernie Brack)

Alongside the Metro station at Jarrow, on the South Shields line, were private sidings for British Steel, where Yorkshire Engine Company 2793 of 1961, BSC No. 53, is seen in January 1986. She was a Janus Class shunter, with a centre cab and two 200 hp Rolls-Royce engines. She later worked at Scunthorpe before being scrapped. (Ernie Brack)

Another new livery is in evidence on 21 June 1986, as Scotrail's No. 47461 stands at Newcastle's former platform 4 with the stock from 1N17, the 00.05 sleeper from King's Cross. Upon arrival the Mk III sleeping cars were shunted into the bay, so that its passengers could have a 'lie-in'. Note that platforms 1–3 have become a car park, a fate that would later befall platforms 4–6. (Dave Jolly)

The second-man's view from the cab of No. 37179 as she approaches Hexham on 9P43, an unfitted ballast train from Tyne Yard to Haydon Bridge on 27 June 1986. The sidings to the left, where we saw No. 31271 earlier, can be seen, but today only the short loop line to the left of the down line remains. The loco was later refurbished as No. 37612 and is currently owned and operated by Direct Rail Services. (Robert Patterson)

On 21 July 1986, Gresley V2 2-6-2 No. 4771 *Green Arrow* worked The Citadel excursion along the Tyne Valley line between Newcastle and Carlisle. She makes a fine sight here running 'wrong line' as she approaches the site of the former Border Counties Junction, where the lines to Allendale and Riccarton Junction once branched off to the south and north respectively. (Colin Alexander)

Metrocar No. 4042 inside South Gosforth depot on 7 September 1986. The articulated cars usually operate in pairs, effectively forming a four-car train. The system opened in 1980 as part of an integrated transport network, with buses, Metro, local trains and ferry under the same operator, with throughfares. Sadly, this ended with deregulation in 1985. The depot was built for the original Tyneside electric fleet in 1923. (Ernie Brack)

Between Gateshead and Blaydon, the River Tyne was heavily industrialised. The NER built Dunston Staithes for the transfer of coal from wagons to ships, and this photograph taken in October 1986 shows the curved rail approach after closure. The staithes, which have listed status, are supposedly the largest wooden structure in Europe and can be seen to this day. (Ernie Brack)

This BR Derby-built Class 108 DMU has been 'cascaded' from the Midland Region and sits in one of the west-end bay platforms at Newcastle next to a Class 08 station pilot, around 1987. Five years earlier, this would have been a '101' or '105' DMU and an '03' shunter. These 'heritage' DMUs of all kinds were on their way out nationally. (Richard Vogel)

Between Tyne Yard and Ouston Junction, near Birtley, No. 56112 waits with 7L06, the 14.29 'merry-go-round' from Tyne Yard to York, as No. 37076 passes hauling HST power car No. 43086 to Leeds Neville Hill on 17 February 1987. The '56' is on the up slow line from which trains could be routed either onto the Consett branch or onto the main line to Durham. (Dave Jolly)

No. 31135 at the now long-closed Simonside wagon repair depot near Jarrow on 17 March 1987. A Class 03 shunter can be seen in the background. Access was along the Jarrow freight branch from Pelaw alongside the South Shields Metro route. Upon closure of the wagon repair shops, the single line was taken over by the Metro, which was able to upgrade to double track. The Jarrow branch was in use for petroleum trains to the oil terminal until 2015. (Robert Patterson)

That same day, No. 31135 is seen at the Jobling Purser bitumen tank sidings at the inaptly-named Paradise on the Elswick branch in Newcastle. The former main line route to Carlisle, which closed in 1982, ran behind the buildings to the left of the locomotive. No. 31135 carries a customised version of the standard livery with the yellow extended around her cab-side windows. Nothing of this scene remains as the site has been redeveloped. (Robert Patterson)

The Birmingham Railway Carriage & Wagon Company's Class 26s were long associated with the Scottish Region but were occasional visitors to Tyneside. No. 26031 is wearing the new Railfreight livery as she climbs from Norwood Junction to join the main line at Low Fell with a train of empty hoppers on 17 July 1987. (Dave Jolly)

An unusual view of Manors on 21 September 1987 with the main line and remains of the old station top right. A twin Metrocar comprising No. 4001, the original prototype, and No. 4085 is climbing out of the underground section on a St James–Pelaw service. The train will cross the Ouseburn on the new Byker viaduct then join the old North Tyne loop at Chillingham Road. (John Carter)

A panoramic view of the King Edward VII Bridge on 29 December 1988 shows No. 37128 on an oil train heading for Newcastle, giving a sense of the sheer size of those spans, four of which total 1,150 feet in length. The opening of the bridge in 1906 meant that Anglo-Scottish trains no longer needed to reverse at Newcastle. (Dave Jolly)

By 1989, the 'heritage' DMUs of the 1950s had been replaced by Sprinters such as Class 156 No. 156462 in Regional Railways livery, which is passing the Tyneside Central Freight Depot with a service towards Sunderland. The electrified line to the left of the picture is the Tyne & Wear Metro route as it burrows under Gateshead. (Richard Vogel)

As well as the Sprinters, Tyneside's suburban passengers from the late 1980s onwards had the dubious pleasure of travelling on the four-wheeled chassis of Pacers such as No. 142519, which is seen passing Felling Metro station. Passengers could interchange between the Metro and trains for Sunderland and Teesside at Heworth, the next station to the east. (Richard Vogel)

Another livery variation is seen outside Gateshead shed in 1989. In 1987, No. 47522 had been painted LNER apple green and named *Doncaster Enterprise*. This locomotive had been rebuilt following serious damage in a collision with a tractor near Perth in 1982. She was originally numbered D1105 and had three spells allocated to Gateshead in the 1970s. She was eventually scrapped in 1998. (Richard Vogel)

A late 1980s view of Heaton Junction shows HST power car No. 43123, with some DMUs and the carriage sheds visible, and the main line curving northwards behind the signal box. No. 43123 was fitted with buffers for temporary use as a Driving Van Trailer when electrified services began with the new Class 91 electric locomotives. (Richard Vogel)

The Stephenson Railway Museum has played host to some notable visitors over the years, including NER P3/LNER J27 No. 2392, Deltic No. 55002 and most memorably, Gresley A4 No. 60019 *Bittern*, seen here inside the former Metro test-track shed in the late 1980s disguised as long-scrapped sister No. 2509 *Silver Link*. The nearby retail park is called Silverlink. (Richard Vogel)

By the late 1980s, Manors station was much rationalised, as can be seen in this view of No. 37251 in grey livery, on a westbound cement train in 1989. The locomotive entered service in 1964, and it was allocated to Gateshead in 1968. By the time of this photograph though, she was a long way from home, being a Cardiff Canton machine. (Richard Vogel)

As the 1980s came to an end, No. 37037 is seen with a train of hoppers from Alcan passing Woodhorn Colliery on 28 May 1989, the year it opened as a museum. The locomotive is carrying the Metals sector livery and the name *Gartcosh*. Fortunately, she survives in preservation at the South Devon Railway. (Dave Jolly)

A National Smokeless Fuels Hunslet 0-6-0 diesel locomotive is seen here at work in the now demolished Monkton Coke Works near Hebburn on Tyneside in 1989, just a year before the plant closed. Monkton's permanently blazing chimney was a prominent landmark for miles around, but like virtually all of Tyneside's traditional industries, it is no more. (Richard Vogel)

Also at Monkton in 1989, ex-BR Class 03 diesel shunter No. 03099, which had spent most of its BR days on Teesside but was withdrawn in 1976, was one of many BR shunters sold for industrial use. Although she appears doomed here, she has been beautifully restored at Peak Rail, Derbyshire by the Heritage Shunters Trust. (Richard Vogel)

Not long before the NCB's electric railway at Westoe closed, to be replaced by a conveyor, we see EE/Baguley electric locomotive No. 13 shunting at Harton staithes on the Tyne on 13 July 1989. This was part of a rabbit warren of sidings that could be viewed from the South Shields ferry landing. A Royal Navy vessel is across the river alongside Smith's Dock at North Shields. (Richard Allen)

As eighty years of electric operation on the Harton system come to an end, NCB No. 13 and a sister perform some of the last duties at St Hilda's sidings, South Shields, in 1989. None of these 1950s-built locomotives made it into preservation, but as well as the three mentioned earlier, E4, built by Siemens in 1909, is at the Stephenson Railway Museum in working order coupled to a wagon full of batteries. (Ian Robinson)

Prototype Tyne & Wear Metrocar No. 4002 stands at a temporary platform at the rear of South Gosforth shed during an open day on 17 September 1989. My Dad worked at the depot as a draughtsman at the time. No. 4001 and No. 4002 had their cab ends modified in line with the eighty-eight production cars, although there are detail differences such as the design of door operating buttons. (Richard Vogel)

Some Pacers were painted in the Tyne & Wear PTE livery to match the Metro fleet, the buses and the Shields ferry. No. 143625 is at platform 12 under John Dobson's magnificent curved roof in Newcastle Central station in 1989. Central was formally opened by Queen Victoria in 1850 and is one of only six Grade 1 listed railway stations in Britain. One of its outstanding features and worth a visit is the former first-class refreshment room, now the Centurion Bar. (Richard Vogel)

Another late 1980s livery variation is seen on No. 47814 as work nears completion on Newcastle Central's new island platform replacing the 'wallside' sidings. Having previously been numbered Nos 47659, 47242 and originally No. D1919, she was subsequently re-engined and became Class 57 No. 57306 *Jeff Tracy*, one of the Virgin 'Thunderbirds'. A '125' in Inter-City livery stands at what was platform 10. (Richard Vogel)

A broadside view of No. 47603 *County of Somerset* as she arrives at Newcastle Central in 1989. Above the centre of the locomotive is the signal box that had replaced several boxes in the re-signalling of 1959, and to the right of that work is in progress on the new footbridge to extend the existing one to the new platforms. The old girder-bridge relay room would disappear in the process. (Richard Vogel)

This is Gateshead Stadium station at the end of the 1980s, and if a comparison is made with the photograph of No. 45052 in April 1982, you can see how dramatically lineside vegetation has taken over since privatisation of the railway. No. 56131 is in charge of a train of 'merry-go-round' hoppers while a Class 08 shunts tank wagons at the TCFD and a Metro 'Supertram' stands at Gateshead Stadium station. (Richard Vogel)

Early signs of East Coast Main Line electrification at Manors in 1989 as No. 31420 passes with a Mk I full brake. There is a solitary mast for overhead wiring on the right. The 'switch-on' took place south from Newcastle in 1990 and to Edinburgh a year later. The rectangular block above the locomotive is Manors Metro station, beyond which a multiplex cinema has been built on the site of New Bridge Street goods station. (Richard Vogel)

Tyneside is widely acknowle
as the birthplace of the ra
Long before 'Railway M
gripped Victorian Britain, pione
engineers on both sides of the
were connecting collieries to the
to assist the export of coal. This
will look at the transitional yea
the North-East's railways, cov
the decline of Tyneside's trad
industries; the closure and lift
many freight lines; and the conv
of Newcastle's suburban netw
the light rapid transit Metro. *Tyr
Railways* also appreciates
renaissance of many of the imp
railway structures of the Nort
and takes a look at some of the
preservation schemes.

Ranging over numerous loc
visiting the suburbs and the be
Tyne Valley to the west anc
travelling slightly further afield
South-East Northumberland co
the book looks at a variety of
power. The photographs co
and captioned by Colin Alex
feature preserved steam ar
diesel traction; steam-, diese
electric-powered locomotives;
Wear Metro stock; and even
fated Advanced Passenger T

AMBERLEY   £14.99

ISBN 978-1-4456-6230-5

9 781445 662305

www.amberley-books.com